SUCCESSFUL SELF-
PUBLISHING

non-fiction

HOW TO SELL A BOOK
ON AMAZON AND LIVE OFF IT!

- Step-by-step guide to selling a book on Amazon -

Kevin Albert

ISBN 979-8402686052

The trouble with the rat race is that even if you win,
you're still a rat.

— LILY TOMLIN

CONTENTS

Introduction

Having dedicated four years of my life to writing my first book and another half a year to publishing it, the moment of truth had arrived. Would all the blood, sweat and tears bear fruit and turn into sales?

I knew that the quality of my book was excellent, both inside – I was solving a latent problem – and outside: the cover, layout, editing, and so on had all been performed by professional experts.

I also knew that I would undoubtedly become a bestselling author, because I had done my research into how to launch a book successfully on Amazon.

But despite all this, the week of publication, when things were going great, I remember remarking to a fellow entrepreneur: "I would love for the book to bring in a hundred dollars a month."

A hundred dollars?!

Knowing that the book I had in my hands was amazing, and that the launch was going to be spectacular... why was I happy to settle for a hundred measly dollars a month? Well, it's because I know the online world very well.

There are some incredible products online that aren't known and don't sell because they are poorly marketed, and there are mediocre products that generate millions (Hawkers sunglasses, for example) because they have good marketing strategies.

Of course, my economic outlook would have been very different had I been prepared to work for my book (create a blog or podcast, deliver conferences, invest in marketing, and so on), but I already had a job that took up all of my time and **what I wanted was for the book to work for me, not the other way around.** I wanted a **100% passive extra income.**

Fortunately, after launching and reaching the "bestseller" position in several Amazon categories, my book continued to sell relatively well and **profits were at around $230 a month**: three times what I had signed up for without hesitating a few months previously.

I was more than happy. A book written out of sheer pig-headedness had shot to the upper ranks on Amazon, ahead of internationally renowned authors. It had improved my personal brand beyond belief – so I was receiving job offers that had been unthinkable before – and I was pocketing over $2000 a year for my vacations.

What more could I want?

I had already achieved much more than what dozens of books on *how to successfully self-publish your book on Amazon* promise.

But a year later, something happened that changed everything: my father retired.

Like many other people his age, my father entered the world of work at a very young age – twelve – and he had not had a single sick day in over fifty years of work, nor had he ever taken more than two weeks' leave in one go. Can you imagine my indignation when I found out that, despite it all, his pension was going to be less than $1000 a month?

$1000 a month after a lifetime of hard graft!

I was incensed, so I decided to utilize my rage constructively.

That was when I decided to find a way for anyone who wrote a book to create a passive income of at least $1000 a month in under a year – not fifty-four years, like my dad.

As a result of this personal mission, involving three years of research and an investment of over $5000 in various training courses, I finally found **a system that enables both writers and non-writers to generate passive income of at least $1000 a month with a single non-fiction book.**

The objective of this book is to allow you to ~~create a decent retirement pension in under a year~~ **ESCAPE THE SYSTEM**.

You heard right. My main aim when writing these words, as I explained in the first part of _Successful Self-Publishing¹_, is to **change the world**. I'm sure you can think of other - maybe even better - ways to do it, but without a doubt

---

¹ soykevinalbert.com/ssp1

helping you to escape the system or "rat race" is a great way to do it.

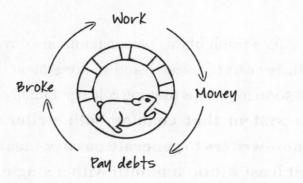

The rat race.

If you know me personally or follow me on social media, I'm sure you know that in addition to writing, I have my fingers in a lot of other pies: most of them projects with the potential to generate much more income than a book can. So...

Why a book?

Why don't I teach you another kind of business that can generate $10,000 or $100,000 a month?

1. A book has enough potential.

You might think $1000 a month is a tiny amount (I do), but that's the pension my father was left with after a lifetime of work.

The objective of this guide is to teach you how to match or beat that figure in under a year, and a book has enough potential to do so.

2. You don't need to invest.

I can't think of any other business where you can invest less than $180 (for the editing, cover and layout) and obtain an income of over $1000 a month.

3. Time.

Getting a retirement pension of $1000 a month may require over fifty years of total dedication. With a book, you can achieve that in under a year with just a few hours' work a week.

4. 100% passive.

Once your book is out there, the income will roll in each month without you having to do anything.

5. 0% risk.

Unlike other types of business, you don't have to quit your day job, risk it all and scrape by until your new project works – if it does at all!

6. You don't need to create a website.

One of the main advantages of online business is that you don't have to rent a physical space in order to operate; a good website is enough.

If you sell your book on Amazon, you don't even need to do that; Amazon will be your website, and it's an amazing one.

7. You don't need to learn about marketing.

In order to sell any product online (or offline), you have to apply a marketing strategy. Whether you decide to outsource or opt for learning to do it yourself, you will have to create a minimum viable **sales funnel**. That means you will need to **attract** users to your product, **convert** those users into leads (potential customers), and **sell them** your product.

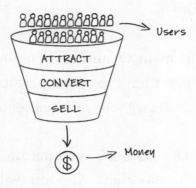

Minimum viable sales funnel.

Amazon takes care of all of these steps without you needing to do anything. And if you want to increase your sales or profits, it has its own marketing platform so you can add more users to the top part of this funnel.

8. You don't need to provide customer service.

Questions, delivery, refunds, complaints... Amazon will take care of it! All you have to worry about is making sure your account number is typed correctly so you can receive your royalties on time.

9. You can repeat the process again and again.

Does $1000 not even cover your mortgage? Then write a second book and double your income, or a third book and triple it, or a fourth... have I made my point?

Creating your first book and reaching this amount monthly may be a real challenge (you're going to have to break through a lot of mental barriers in the process), but once you've done it, you'll see it all from a different perspective and I'm sure you'll be spurred on to write the next one – this time, dedicating much less time to it.

10.   It's a good *first step*.

Even if, like me, your dabbling in the online world goes beyond writing or earning $1000 a month, a book is a great starting point:

- It will enable you to create a real empire based on your work if you decide to use it as a means to position yourself as an expert **in your field** and attract customers to sell your products or services to.

- It will give you the confidence you need to tackle a new, more ambitious business **in another** field. When you see that it's possible to generate income without relying on a boss, your fears will be less likely to cause you to throw in the towel halfway and go back to the "security" of a traditional job.

And now that you know that freedom awaits you once you escape the system thanks to a single book...

It's time to sell your book!

Bestseller in 24 hours

Have you ever been impressed by hearing that a friend or acquaintance was a bestselling author? Have you felt some healthy – or not so healthy – envy for that person? Did you think it was a feat only a select few with the gift of writing could ever hope to achieve? Did you think it was something you yourself could never manage?

I've got great news for you!

Not only can **you be a bestselling author on Amazon,** you can get there **in less than 24 hours!**

Yep, I'm telling you the truth. I promise. If I'm not, I'll invite you round for dinner.

So how do you do it?

This may surprise you, but Amazon recalculates the position of all the books on its platform **each hour and for each category**. This means that, if your book *just happens* to be the most sold in a given category on a single day... **Amazon will give it a "bestseller" badge**.

Now we know that reaching bestselling position on Amazon depends on just two factors – your book's **categories** and its **sales in 24 hours** – you can prepare a launch strategy that guarantees you'll achieve this recognition.

Launch strategy

For this launch strategy, we will be focusing on the digital (Kindle) version of your book, for several reasons:

- It's better to focus your energies.

- The digital version allows you to use some good marketing tools and strategies.
- The physical version will benefit from the achievements of its digital brother, as both will appear linked on Amazon.

11. Put your book on preorder.

Approximately **one month before** the date on which you want to publish your book, I recommend putting it on preorder with KDP. This is as easy as checking a box and indicating your chosen publication date.

Pre-order

I am ready to release my book now

⊙ **Make my Kindle eBook available for Pre-order.** Is KDP Pre-order right for me? ⌄

Set Release Date (GMT)
01/25/2022

Although it's an optional step, doing it this way will enable you to benefit from the advantages of

Kindle Countdown Deals[2], (as long as your launch is happening in a market that allows it), as we'll see later on.

12.   Request your categories.

Within hours of putting your book on preorder, you will be assigned an ASIN number, which you can see from your KDP dashboard:

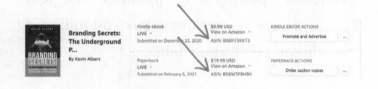

Location of the ASIN on the KDP dashboard.

Once you have this number, you can request the categories for your book.

---

[2] One of the two types of promotion, along with the *free book* promotion we can run when we sign our book up with the KDP Select program.

But how do you find the best categories with the most potential to turn your work into a bestseller?

It's simple – all you need to do is follow three steps:

(If you've read the <u>second part of Successful Self-Publishing</u>[3], you can skip this bit)

1. Find the possible categories for your book.

To find these possible categories, head to the "Product details" section of similar books to yours (they may be in direct competition with you or not) and note down the categories these appear under. You'll see that each book is included in two or three different categories.

---

[3] soykevinalbert.com/ssp2

Product details
ASIN : B08R73RXT3
Publication date : February 14, 2021
Language : English
File size : 1594 KB
Print length : 227 pages
Lending : Enabled
Best Sellers Rank: #66,713 in Kindle Store (See Top 100 in Kindle Store)
    #3 in Home-Based Business Advertising
    #4 in Outsourcing (Kindle Store)
    #7 in Global Marketing (Kindle Store)
Customer Reviews: ★★★★☆ ˅   53 ratings

Location of categories under "Product details".

Try to make a list of at least 15 possible categories.

2. Find out the nº1 book in each category.

Now that you have your list of possible categories, it's time to find out which have the best chance of turning your book into a bestseller.

To do this, first go to the list of the bestselling books in each of these categories by clicking on the name of each category in the "Product details" section of each book you're researching.

Once you're in, click on the nº1 book for each of these categories and note down its ABSR. This is the ABSR you'll have to beat in order to become a bestseller in that category. The higher the ABSR, the easier you'll find it to reach n°1.

Product details
ASIN : B08R73RXT3
Publication date : February 14, 2021
Language : English
File size : 1594 KB
Print length : 227 pages
Lending : Enabled
Best Sellers Rank: #66,713 in Kindle Store (See Top 100 in Kindle Store)
#3 in Home-Based Business Advertising
#4 in Outsourcing (Kindle Store)
#7 in Global Marketing (Kindle Store)
Customer Reviews: ★★★★☆ ▾ 53 ratings

Location of the ASBR under "Product details".

3. Prepare your list of categories.

With this small amount of research, you'll know which categories are the most suitable for your book's topic, and – most important of all – which have the best chances of getting you to bestseller position: those with the highest ABSR.

So far so good, but when you start uploading your book to KDP and you come to the section where you need to select your two categories, you may be surprised to find one of your chosen categories is not on the list.

But don't panic – you didn't waste your time. Amazon has a lot of categories to select from when uploading your book to KDP. In any case, all you have to do is select the two that best suit those you chose during your research phase, and once your book is published, email Amazon customer support to ask them nicely to include your book in the categories you didn't manage to find. They'll deal with it for you within forty-eight hours.

Pro tip: As I mentioned before, when you upload your book to KDP, you'll have the option of selecting two categories – but did you know you can actually **put your book into ten different categories?** Can you imagine the impact this could have on your sales?!

So, what do you need to do to get your book listed in more than two categories? Simple: ask. Go to the contact section of KDP and write to them to ask for your book to be added to the list of ten categories you prepared, for both your book's digital and physical versions.

This is what I usually write:

Hi,

I would like my book with ASIN: XXX (Kindle) and ASIN: XXX (paperback) to be included in the following categories:

Kindle

"Kindle Store > Kindle eBooks > Education & Reference"

"Kindle Store > Kindle eBooks > Business & Investing"

"Kindle Store> Kindle eBooks > Language, linguistics and writing"

...

Paperback

"Books > Reference > Writing, Research & Publishing Guides"

"Books > Business & Economics > Small Business & Entrepreneurship"

"Books > Self-Help > Creativity"

(And so on.)

13.   Prepare your launch team.

Your *launch team* is basically going to consist of a group of family and friends who are prepared to buy your book within 48 hours of its launch[4]. Some of them will do it because they're interested in the topic and really want to read the book, others because they're proud to own a book you wrote, others simply to support you... It doesn't matter why they do it, but the bigger your launch team, the better. Of course, if you have followers or fans you want to add to this group, then go ahead.

Try to get at least 20 people on this team. The higher the number, the more positions you'll climb in Amazon's ranks, and the more effective your launch will be.

---

[4] I recommend doing the launch around a week after your book is published, so you can take advantage of the boost Amazon gives new books in their first few days.

Becoming a bestseller in a subcategory is not the same as doing it in a main category. And, I repeat, this is going to depend on the sales you can obtain within 24 hours.

It's important to have your team prepared in advance, but don't go crazy, obviously; two or three weeks is more than enough. Explain as much of it to them as you think is necessary, but above all, don't forget to tell them their main mission will be to buy the book **on the day you ask them to**, that is, the first day of your launch.

IMPORTANT: I'm sure a lot of people on your launch team will want to buy the physical version of your book so that you can sign it and they can put it on their favorite bookshelf where everyone can see it, but you need to make it clear to them that **their task is to buy the digital version**. If they want to buy both, then great – but first things first.

14.   Select your marketing platforms.

In most markets, having a launch team of around twenty people is enough to reach the top position in one or more of the categories you've requested on Amazon. However, if your target market is Amazon.com, things are a little more difficult. This isn't a bad thing; it means that more (far more) books are sold in the US than in any other market, so if you do things right, you can earn more (far more) money. So, let's do things right.

Luckily for us, there are many platforms in the US that enable you to promote your book during its launch.

Using the services of one of these platforms is as simple as filling out the details of your book, choosing the day you want to promote it on, and paying the corresponding fee.

You'll encounter fees for everyone's budget: from free to prohibitive, such as over $500. Usually, the results you'll obtain will vary in accordance with the price you pay – but be careful! That's not always the case.

To avoid buying a pig in a poke and to be as safe as possible, I recommend choosing your platform from the exhaustive list compiled by *Reedsy*:

soykevinalbert.com/promo-platforms

For my US launches, I usually choose four or five platforms and try not to invest more than $170 in total.

To optimize my investment, rather than concentrating all my promotions on one day (something Amazon doesn't seem to favor), I configure each platform for a different day, making sure they coincide with my Kindle Countdown Deal.

For the first day of your Countdown Deal, you don't need to hire a promotion platform, as that's the day you'll be making good use of your launch team.

15.   Configure your Kindle Countdown Deal.

As you will know if you read the second instalment of *Successful Self-Publishing*, this type of promotion enables you to sell your book at a discounted price for a limited period of time. Customers will be able to see its usual price alongside the promotional one on the book details page, as well as a clock showing the time remaining for the promotional price.

All you have to do is select a **start date** and an **end date** (with a maximum of seven days in between), the **number of price increases** (with a maximum of five) and the **starting price**.

In your case, I recommend setting your Countdown Deal for five to seven days (depending on the marketing platforms you decide to use) a week after your book's publication date, with a starting price of 99c and just one price increase. This means that your book will be available for 99c for the days you set the promotion for, and then return to its usual price.

IMPORTANT: In order to activate a Countdown Deal a week after publication, do not skip the first step – preorder – as your book must have been signed up to KDP Select for at least 30 days before starting your promotion.

Running a Countdown Deal during your launch serves two purposes:

1. **Increasing your sales**: both your organic sales, including those of your launch team, and those from the marketing

platforms you decided to use. A discounted price along with the urgency created by the timer Amazon puts just above it will have immense power.

2. **Increasing your profits**: Unlike if you manually reduced your book to 99c instead of using a Kindle Countdown Deal, your royalties will not be reduced to 30% but rather will stay at their usual 70%.

16.   Launch your book.

It's time for your launch; day 1 of your Countdown Deal.

It's time to get your launch team into action.

You can contact them however you prefer: via WhatsApp, email, phone... What matters is that you ensure they get your message that same day, and that you notify everyone at the same time.

Don't divide this task up and tell a few people in the morning, others in the afternoon, and others in the evening. Sit down and don't get up until you've finished the task.

C'est fini!

If you follow these simple steps, **I guarantee you will reach bestseller position** in one or more of the ten categories you requested.

Pro tip: if you want to know the number of books you need to sell in twenty-four hours in order to reach the top position in your main or favorite category, take a look at *Publisher Rocket:*

soykevinalbert.com/rocket

Sales in 24 hours in order to reach n° 1

Checklist and timeline.

Given the importance of following these six steps in the correct order and at the right time, I have prepared for you a checklist and corresponding timeline.

One month before publication:

☐ 1. Put your book on preorder.

Three weeks before publication:

☐ 2. Request your categories.
☐ 3. Prepare your launch team.
☐ 4. Select your promotional platforms.

The week of publication:

☐ 5. Set up your Kindle Countdown Deal.

One week after publication:

☐ 6. Launch your book.

So, now that you're a bestseller, and before moving on to the next chapter, I have some bad news for you...

Being a bestseller won't do you any good.

During my research, I invested nearly $600 in a course that promised to teach us how to become Amazon bestsellers. I have to say that, although I ended up cursing the conman who sold me the course, it did deliver on its promise. That is to say that it taught exactly what I myself have just taught you in barely ten pages, but in video format and for around **100 times the price of this book** (and we've barely even begun).

It was my mistake, and I've observed that it's very common. Until recently, when I heard the word "bestseller", I associated it with sales (a lot of them) and money. However, the reality is different: become a bestseller on Amazon (without a good strategy behind you) does nothing more than inflate your ego and kid those naïve people who still think it equals success.

So, did I tell you this whole tale about how to become a bestselling author on Amazon just so that I could laugh at you, like the people who sold me that course? No.

Reaching this position, especially during your first few weeks after publication and with a strategy for afterward, is a fundamental step to succeeding in your work – which, in my view, consists of **selling a lot of books, getting a lot of income from them, and doing this over a sustained period of time**.

But don't be fooled – you don't achieve this by being a bestseller for a day. You need to be what is called a **longseller.**

From bestseller to longseller

You can be a longseller without being a bestseller and vice versa, but I haven't taught you a strategy that guarantees you will reach bestseller position during your book's launch just to fill the pages up. As I said, **being a bestseller with a strategy for afterward** is a potent catalyst for the success of your book, because if you do things right, **it can generate sufficient momentum** to maintain sales in the long term. It is this – not getting that "best seller" badge – that I want to teach you with this book: how to obtain a good passive income every month and make it last your whole life.

"Best seller" badge on search page.

It's important that you don't fall into the trap of thinking that if your book is a bestseller during its launch, your work here is done and you can just sit back and watch the sales keep rolling in. Let me insist one more time: this strategy is only useful for giving you the momentum you need to get started, but on its own it's not worth anything:

I know a couple of gurus who, with their list of over 20,000 subscribers, performed a launch that not only enabled them to position their book as a bestseller in the best categories but actually reached nᵒ 1 on all of Amazon... with a sh*tty book. The following week, it had dropped off the map, and the few genuine sales they were getting were receiving nothing but bad reviews complaining about the quality. It did these two gurus absolutely no good whatsoever to get their book as the top seller on all of Amazon, and just a few months later, they ended up pulling it.

An even more noteworthy case is that of the *non-writer* Brent Underwood, an American marketing consultant who, with the sole aim of proving the worthlessness of becoming an Amazon bestseller, published a one-page book containing a picture of a foot entitled *Putting My Foot Down*[5] – and got it to be an Amazon bestseller in under five minutes.

I recommend that you google Underwood's story, but if you feel too lazy to do that then

---

[5] soykevinalbert.com/pmfd

here are two extracts from interviews with him after his feat:

- «People get to the top of a category and, even if it only lasts an hour, they make sure they mention it in all their bios and they brag about it for the rest of their lives.»
- «There are all kinds of shameful websites promising secrets, tricks, conferences and online seminars for becoming a bestseller overnight.»

Now that you're clear on that reaching bestselling position is simply an intermediary step on your way to becoming a real longseller and increasing your income, let's move on to the next step.

The 7 keys to becoming a longseller

For your book to become a longseller, it's as "easy" as this: after its launch, it must continue to achieve a considerable number of sales. For this to happen, there are 3 requirements or stages: your book being shown (visibility), your book piquing people's interest, and your book selling.

Fortunately for you, with Amazon, you have the power to directly impact each of these 3 stages, bearing in mind 7 key points:

1. The title.

No matter how good your book is, it's no use if your readers can't find it. That's why I consider the title to be the n° 1 secret to a book's success, as it's **the main deciding factor in whether or not Amazon displays your book** when a user searches for something.

Formula for a perfect title[6] that both Amazon and your potential readers will love:

---

[6] Explained step by step in the first instalment of Successful Self-Publishing: soykevinalbert.com/ssp1

FPT = keywords (SEO) + solution (sore point) + personality + time limit

2. The cover.

If the title is the main factor in helping readers find your book, then without a doubt the cover is the **main factor in capturing their interest**. A well-designed cover – designed for sale – will attract users' attention and get you more clicks than the competition.

In addition, if Amazon's algorithm detects that your book is getting more clicks, it will assume that it is relevant to readers and move it up the ranks, which will give it even more visibility.

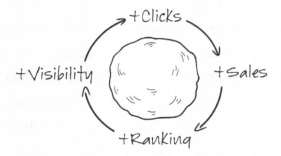

Snowball effect

Given that the cover will play such an important role in your book's success, you need to take it seriously. By this I mean that you are not going to design it yourself, nor is it going to come from your brother-in-law who's great at drawing, or your cousin with an Art degree...

Say it with me: **my book's cover must be designed by a professional**.

3. The description.

Once a user clicks on your book's icon in the search results or Amazon recommendations, they will be redirected to the product page: a page that Amazon has prepared solely for your book. There, the user can obtain absolutely all the information they need in order to decide whether to buy it. Among all this information, the element with the most persuasive power is, without a doubt, your book's description. A description written using persuasive language and presented in a format that your potential readers enjoy.

4. Look inside.

If your description isn't convincing enough to close the sale, the next element your prospective reader can use to help them make the decision is the "look inside" option.

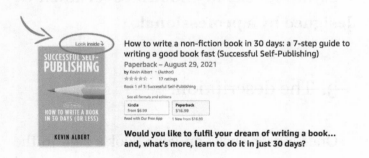

How to write a non-fiction book in 30 days: a 7-step guide to writing a good book fast (Successful Self-Publishing)
Paperback – August 29, 2021
by Kevin Albert ~ (Author)
★★★★★ ˅   17 ratings
Book 1 of 3: Successful Self-Publishing

See all formats and editions

Kindle	Paperback
from $6.99	$16.99
Read with Our Free App	1 New from $16.99

Would you like to fulfil your dream of writing a book... and, what's more, learn to do it in just 30 days?

Location of the "look inside" option.

This feature is the digital equivalent of flicking through the pages of a book in a bookshop; it enables the reader to see the first few pages, 10%[7] to be precise, before deciding whether or not to buy it. Being aware of this will allow you to optimize your content in order to:

- Increase your percentage of sales.
- Get the email addresses of those who can't decide.

Increase your percentage of sales

Managing to increase the number of users who end up buying your book after using the "look inside" feature is as simple as applying these two basic strategies:

---

[7] You can write to KDP and request that this percentage is modified if you want.

1. **Take care over your contents page**. The contents page is the most-visited part of a non-fiction book, so in addition to creating it as early as possible, it's important that you take care to redact the chapters in an appealing way. Treat your chapters like you would your book's title.

2. **Get straight to the heart of the matter**. After your contents page, get straight to the content. **Demonstrate as soon as you can that your book is worth reading**. It's important that you don't leave the best till last and that you don't repeat what you've already said in your description or add sections that Amazon already has specific places for, such as your bio, which goes on your author page.

Get the email addresses of those who can't decide

It's highly like that, if the user leaves your book's page without completing checkout, you've lost that sale forever. That's why it's a great idea to use these first few pages to get their email addresses by offering them something in return: a free resource, access to a private video relating to your book's topic, an invitation to a webinar[8], or similar.

Having the contact details of these undecided users means you can put into practice hundreds of strategies that will enable you to increase your profits to a point you're happy with. Although this is something on the level of a master's in digital marketing, the simple act of sending an email from time to time to your list of contacts and talking about some interesting topic relating to your book's subject **will improve your sales for minimal effort**.

5. Author's page.

---

[8] The term *webinar* is a neologism combining the words *web* and *seminar*. It refers to any content in video format whose main objective is educational and practical.

In my time as a businessman, I learned (the difficult way) something I'll remember forever:

*To get a sale, you need to sell not just the product but also your company and **yourself**.*

The lack of any of these three elements will prevent the sale from taking place, especially when we're talking about products with a higher price.

On a platform like Amazon, we don't need to sell the company – we're already talking about the company with the best customer ratings in the world. So, if you do a good job selling your product via the correct application of the key components of this chapter, all that's left to do is **sell yourself** – and the right tool to do this with is your author page on Amazon.

The author page is the equivalent of the "about us" or "about me" section of a corporate website or personal blog. It's no coincidence that it's the page **most visited by users**: your customers need to know who you are.

You should use this section to forge a connection with your readers, generate trust, transmit professionalism... In short, to let people see the person behind the pages of the book(s) they are reading or thinking of reading.

Don't make the mistake of using your author page as a kind of resumé.

On certain occasions, mentioning your academic credentials may be advisable or even necessary – but the most important thing, and your main aim when filling out this section, is to empathize with your reader. If you can get them to identify with you and your story, they will be able to imagine themselves achieving the same things: the achievements you describe reaching with your book. If you can do this, the sale is guaranteed.

But be careful! Don't invent a backstory just because you think it will sell better. That's a short-term strategy that may end up biting you in the butt later.

Many sellers of multilevel companies (such as Herbalife, to name one at random) hire cars and luxury houses just so they can take a selfie to post to their social media and grab a few foolhardy followers taken in by the so-called high life these conmen peddle by selling chocolate milkshakes. They are so cheesy that they even sometimes hire these luxuries in pools of several couples (for some reason, they love to show happy couples) and take turns to have their pictures taken.

This type of lie may be somewhat useful for a period of time within the world of multilevel marketing or new infoproducers (they both use exactly the same strategies), but on Amazon you'll get caught out before you know it, and the house of cards will come tumbling down.

Now that you know why this section is important and how to make the most of it, let's move on to the technical part.

Unlike the other elements, your author page isn't filled in via your KDP dashboard. That's why many authors skip this step – whether out of laziness or obliviousness – which enables you to differentiate yourself and earn a lot of Brownie points in the eyes of Amazon and your readers.

The first step to creating your author page is to open an account with *Amazon Author Central*: *authorcentral.amazon.com*.

Once you've signed up, you'll find several sections at your disposal for turning your readers into your fans. That's right – as an author, you can have your own followers on Amazon.

Don't settle for just uploading your photo and bio: if you have a blog, don't hesitate to link to it, and if you have one or more videos where you present your book or talk about topics related to it, like a talk or conference you delivered, upload them! Let your readers see how you speak and express yourself – it will massively increase the degree of connection and trust they have in you. This is exactly what we want.

Note: if you upload a new book to Amazon having already created your author page, then for it to be shown on your profile you need to add it manually by going to the "Books" tab at the top and clicking "Add more books".

Location of "Add more books".

6. Your book itself (obviously).

Did you think that by applying a series of tricks and strategies, you could live off a crappy book? I have both good and bad news for you.

First, the bad news: that's not going to happen.

And now, the good news: unlike with fiction books, the success of a non-fiction book lies principally in whether it delivers on its promise. It may have spelling mistakes, be difficult to follow, read repetitively... but if the reader finishes your book having found the solution to the problem they were trying to resolve, you will have a satisfied reader.

I mean, do you really think that if I demonstrate with this book that it's possible to generate **a retirement pension in under a year** instead of in fifty years, anyone is going to be unhappy because I made a spelling error or because they don't like my jokes?

As you can see, in addition to having a good book, becoming a longselling author is as easy as...

- Getting found (**attracting**);
- Getting clicked on once you've been found (**converting**);
- Getting bought once you've been clicked on (**selling**).

In other words: you need to create a mini sales funnel where you have control over the effectiveness of each of its levels thanks to the 7 key points we just looked at:

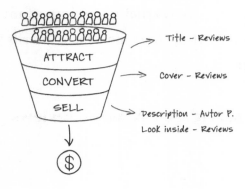

Main role of each of the 7 key points on each level.

As you can see in the image, although each element is interrelated, they each play a specific role on one of the three levels.

Did you notice there was one element repeated on every level and which I also "forgot" to mention in the list of 7 key points?

As I'm sure you can imagine, I didn't forget. The fact I saved it till last when I really should have made it the third thing I talked about – since it's the third element our potential reader will encounter – shows that it's so important when it comes to getting the sale that it merits its own chapter.

I'm talking about **Amazon reviews**.

Reviews:
the key to success

The reviews of a book carry a lot of the responsibility for an author's success or failure. And given that Amazon is the world leader in selling books, getting real reviews on the platform is essential.

Not many things hurt more than going through the difficult process of writing, publishing and launching a book just to see it achieve barely any sales and end up forgotten due to a lack of reviews.

Think about it: how many times have you bought a book without taking a look at the reviews? I don't know about you, but nowadays

Amazon makes it so easy that I don't buy anything without reading a few comments from previous buyers or readers first.

Don't throw away all the work you dedicated to your book by missing out such an important aspect, because **getting the first reviews of your book is your responsibility.**

Why are they so important?

1. Credibility and social proof

When we search for a product, choose a restaurant, find a hotel to stay in or buy a book, we all look at the reviews and ratings.

A product with a lot of positive reviews on Amazon and an average rating of 4-5 stars gives us peace of mind when purchasing. We think that, if there are so many people satisfied with it, we probably won't be disappointed either. And in the case of a non-fiction book, **reviews tell us it really will fulfil its promise**.

This takes on extra importance when we're comparing two similar products. Imagine that one product had dozens – or hundreds – of positive 5-star reviews, while the other had none (or worse, had 1- to 3-star reviews), which would you pick?

A book with no reviews is not necessarily a bad book, but compared to a similar book with a large number of positive comments underneath it, the chances of the first being chosen by readers drop off drastically.

2. They influence Amazon's algorithm

Amazon, just like Google or YouTube, is a big search engine.

When people use it, the first results they see are determined by its internal algorithm, and reviews are an important part of this: they help you to improve your ranking.

The better your ranking, the more chance of people finding you – and the more chance of them finding you, the more likely you are to sell your book.

3. They drive sales

Each review you receive will improve your ranking, boost your credibility and attract potential readers who are more inclined to believe in the virtues of your book if they're mentioned by a third party (readers) than if you talk about them yourself.

On top of all this, there are several platforms – such as BookBub, Kindle Nation Daily and The Fussy Librarian – that will allow you to market your book for free once you reach a minimum number of reviews (between 5 and 10, with a rating of over 3.5-4 stars). This way, once you reach that threshold, you will have new opportunities to market (and sell) your book thanks to its reviews.

Warning: don't attempt trickery

Before explaining to you how to get these valuable Amazon reviews, it's important that you know **what you CAN'T do**.

Amazon has a zero-tolerance policy toward reviews designed to mislead or manipulate customers. Ignoring these rules may lead to the misleading review being simply deleted, or to your book being permanently removed from Amazon's catalog – or, worse, to your author profile being permanently closed with no recourse. And if you're living off your book, this is the equivalent of being fired from your company overnight with no appeal or redundancy pay, so BE CAREFUL.

Here is a list of the things you cannot doing when obtaining a review:

1. Pay or otherwise incentivize someone to leave a review.
2. Offer a gift for reviewing.
3. Offer a refund.
4. Swap reviews with other authors.

Finally, in the same way that misleading reviews in favor of your book are punished, bad reviews against books by your competition are also disallowed. Although there are still many "authors" (for want of a better word) who use this despicable technique, if Amazon or the author in question realize it's happening, the trickster may find themselves with a deleted account before they can blink.

Now that you know what you can't do, let's look at what's allowed in order to increase your book's reviews quickly and legitimately.

How to get reviews on Amazon

As a self-published author, having a good number of positive reviews on Amazon from the start can catapult your launch and make your work stand out above the competition.

That's why I want to highlight the importance of not considering publication complete until you've got these initial reviews. The more (real) positive reviews, the better, but **getting between 10 and 20 your first month after launching** is a good goal to aim for.

There are many strategies for finding readers prepared to leave a rating, but some take a lot of time... and money. There are platforms that sell them for around $200 each (complying with Amazon rules).

So, to get reviews during your book's launch or add them to a book you already published, we're going to look at **5 highly effective strategies** that won't require you to waste your money or your time.

1. Your launch team.

Having a good launch team will not only enable you to reach the top positions on Amazon when you publish your book, but it will also help consolidate you as a longselling author thanks to, among other things, the reviews this strategy can bring you in the first few days.

Generally speaking, getting half the members of your launch team to leave you a review is quite a feat. The main reasons some people might not do it include:

- They didn't like your book.
- They didn't read your book.
- They can't be bothered.
- They forget.

So, to try and ensure at least 50% reviews, and not to end up frustrated and annoyed, follow these steps:

1. **Don't send group messages/emails**: If you're going to ask someone to spend their time writing a review for your book, the least you can do is spend your time writing to or calling that person directly. Firstly, out of simple **courtesy and respect** (your time is no more valuable than theirs), and secondly because they will feel **more committed** if you write to them personally than if you send a group WhatsApp, where they might think: "Out of all these people, they won't notice if I don't do it".

2. **Do an audit of your team**: Create a simple spreadsheet with the names of all your team members, so you can check:

- If you notified them that your book was available for sale.
- If they bought it.
- If you asked them to leave a review.
- If they left one.

This way, you ensure no one escapes your notice and that you don't keep bugging those who already did their bit. Because, yes, you are going to have to bug people a little.

3. **Ask them to let you know**: Ask the members of your team to tell you once they've left their review, so that you can read it carefully. In addition to generating extra commitment, this will show them that you truly value their comments and that their opinion matters to you.

4. They don't have to read the whole book: One of the main reasons someone on your team might not leave you a review is that they haven't finished reading your book yet or even that they don't plan to read it at all, whether because they don't have time or because they're not particularly interested in the topic. It's important to free them of this pressure by explaining that it's not necessary, that they can have an opinion on what they have read so far, and that if they want, they can modify their review later.

If you follow these steps, I promise that you will multiply the number of reviews you receive from your launch team.

2. Find reviewers on Amazon.

This method may require considerable time and effort, but if you didn't reach the number of reviews you had set with your team, it's a good alternative to keep getting reviews, at least until you reach that objective.

There are many ways to find reviewers who are prepared to give you a rating. Let's look at my favorite two:

1. List of main reviewers.

There is a <u>list of the top 1000 Amazon reviewers</u>[9]. Not only have these top reviewers left hundreds (sometimes thousands) of reviews on Amazon products, but they also tend to be very detailed and elaborate. That's why we're so interested in getting a review from one of them, as they are able to attract lots of readers/sales.

To choose the reviewers you're going to contact, you will have to do a little research by going into their profiles and noting down

---

[9] amazon.com/reviews/top-reviewers

those who have left reviews on other books in your genre or field.

However! Not all these profiles will have their contact details visible. Your goal is to find at least 20 candidates you can contact, whether by email, through their website, or on social media.

Contact details.

2. Reviewers of similar books.

The alternative option goes in precisely the opposite direction: instead of starting with the profiles of reviewers and then finding out whether they've left reviews on similar books, you can start with the reviews of other books to find good reviewers (who have no reason not to be on the list of top reviewers).

It couldn't be easier. Go to the ten best books in your field and scroll to their reviews. You will see that, by default, they appear in order of importance: those at the top received the most "useful" votes from other readers. Choose a few of the most upvoted and go to those reviewers' profiles by clicking on their names.

As with the previous, your objective is to note down at least 20 possible reviewers with their contact details visible.

Pro tip: given that Amazon makes it increasingly harder to view contact information for commenters and it could drive you to distraction trying to get those 20 candidates you want to contact, I recommend trying the KDROI tool, which, among other interesting features, will enable you to scan tens of thousands of commenters' profiles and get their contact details **in a matter of seconds**:

soykevinalbert.com/kdroi

Now that you have prepared your list, it's time to contact them – by email, if possible – and cross your fingers that they get back to you.

You can use this template:

Hi [reader's name]:

I read your review of the book [book title] on Amazon, and when I went into your profile, I saw that you had reviewed several books in the same style.

[Explain to them why you liked their review. Maybe it was because it was detailed, sincere, or original]. This is why I wanted to talk to you about my own book.

[Tell them about your book, include a link to it on Amazon and tell them how their rating can benefit other readers].

It would be a pleasure if I could send you a copy and/or a PDF and you could let me know what you think.

Thanks in advance,

[Your name]

If you still haven't had a reply after a week, don't get stressed out. Many of these people receive requests like yours on a daily basis and be working their way through their inboxes. Let a few more days go by, and write to them again, asking if they received your email and if they are interested in writing a review of a free copy of your book.

If they agree to do it, be patient. Remember that they agreed to read your book as a favor to you.

3. Ask for a review at the end of your book.

Not many readers realize just how important reviews are to us as authors. I'm sure that lots of people who enjoyed your book would be happy to leave a review if you just gave them a little nudge in the right direction.

And given that Amazon doesn't provide the email addresses or other contact details of our readers, we need to give them that nudge from within the book itself. Keep it concise and brief and remind readers to let you know what they thought. The best place to do this is in the last few pages, since good reviews tend to come from people who read the book all the way to the end.

Simply making this request will double the number of reviews you get. If you do it right, the proportion of comments left on each book read will go through the roof.

How to ask for a review?

1. Focus on giving.

There's nothing wrong with asking for a review, but if you want to get something, first you should offer something.

CAREFUL: I'm not talking about giving a gift in return for a review, as this is against Amazon's terms. I'm talking about having offered your readers a good book that entertained, excited, and inspired them... or, in the case of a non-fiction book, which **delivered on its promise**.

2. Emphasize the importance of their review.

In order for your reader to take the initiative, they need to understand that their review is important to:

- **Improve the book**: Explain that it will help you improve future editions of your book – or other books – if you can get their feedback.

- **Help other readers**: Emphasize the usefulness of a review to enable other readers to find your book and know what to expect from it.

3. **Humanize your request.**

Find a way to remind readers that there is a real person – not a big publishing company – behind the pages of your book, with real emotions and feelings. Tell them how hard the journey to finishing your book was, and how excited you are to be able to share it with others. By doing this, you can **get people to leave a review *for you*** as well as for your book.

Pro tip: As you know, a picture is a worth a thousand words, right? A quick and effective way to humanize yourself is to upload a non-professional picture of yourself in your request for a review. Show a side of your private life you think you readers could relate to or identify with: a family photo, a picture of your pet, you doing your favorite hobby (if this happens to be taxidermy, maybe go for the family photo instead...)

4. Just one request.

Many authors use the last few pages of their book to make all kinds of requests:

- Sign up to my newsletter.
- Follow me on social media (featuring seven links to their "main" socials).
- Buy my course or my other books.
- Hire my services.
- Leave me a review.
- ...

These are all good calls to action to end your book with, but if you don't want to overload your reader with so many requests that they don't end up doing any of them, **pick just one**.

Personally, I recommend that you always begin by requesting a review, and if once you reach a considerable number of reviews, you change it to your next favorite request. If you have more books, that one would be my second option.

Note: In the Kindle version, you can choose a different request from the start, since the system itself will suggest to the reader that they rate your book. This way, you will also avoid sounding repetitive.

5. Share the direct link to your reviews

Many authors, when asking for a review, include a link to their book's page in order to make the reader's task easier. Although this will go some way to increasing your conversion, it puts the onus on the reader to find the review page, and lots of well-intentioned people will throw in the towel before finding it and leaving their comments.

What if there were a way to include a link directly to the review page? All they would have to do is click and start typing.

There is, and it's really simple:

1. Depending on the format you want to direct your reader to – physical or digital – find the corresponding ASIN.

2. Add the chosen ASIN to the following link:

amazon.com/review/create-review?&asin=

Pro tip 1: Use a URL shortener. If you want your URL to look prettier (which will translate into higher conversion) you can use a URL shortener such as _Bitly_[10].

Pro tip 2: Create a QR code. Particularly for the physical version of your book, in addition to using a URL shortener, it might be worth converting it into a QR code[11]. Put yourself in the reader's shoes: imagine you're on the beach, reading a paperback, and the author suddenly suggests that you visit a website. What would be easier for you: to type a website address into your smartphone browser, or to go straight there by using your phone's camera?

4. Get your readers' email addresses.

As I mentioned above, Amazon does not provide any contact information for our readers

---

[10] _bitly.com_
[11] I use _codigos-qr.com_

(in my opinion, this is one of the biggest drawbacks to selling on this platform). This means that, unless a customer writes to us first, we have no way of getting in touch with them.

But **what if we could get our readers' email addresses?**

Well, first of all, having waited a reasonable length of time, we could write to them to ask what they thought of the book and **encouraging them to write a review**.

So, **how do you get them?**

Well, as always, by giving before expecting to receive. So, the first thing you need to do is think about what you can offer your readers that's sufficiently appealing – without going overboard – to convince them to give you their email address in return.

It could be access to an educational video or videos, attendance at one of your webinars, the audio version of your book, an Excel template, or similar.

Once you've decided what to offer your readers, you need to let them know that in order to access this free resource, all they have to do is drop you an email asking for it.

There are several ways of automatizing this process, but until you start receiving so many requests that it takes you more than an hour each week to reply to them, doing it this way will be enough. But if you do want to learn how to automatize the process from the start, drop me an email at _books@soykevinalbert.com_ with the subject header _Automatization_. KIDDING ;)

Finally, **where should you put this message?**

It's easy. If you put your request for reviews at the end of your book, put your request for emails at the beginning, if you can, or at the end of the chapter that relates to the free resource you intend to offer.

Now that you have your customers' contact details, **use them responsibly**. Although the readers gave you their express permission to contact them, always try to follow this rule:

Only contact your readers if you have something to offer them.

In the first email you send, it's easy to use the excuse that you're interested in what they thought of the book and want to clear up any doubts they might have before asking them to leave a review. But if you don't get a review from them after this and you want to ask for one again, think carefully about what your second email will offer them before you write it. If you can't think of anything, I'm sorry, but you can't bother them again.

5. Relaunch your book

A great way to give your book's sales an extra push while getting a good number of fresh reviews is to do a relaunch.

This simply consists of **getting together a new launch team** and, if you want, including a new chapter or update (one that adds value, of course). This way, not only will you get those new reviews you want, but you will also climb back up Amazon's rankings, which in turn will attract more sales.

Note: This strategy is perfect for writers who want to revive a book they had already published on Amazon before they read this guide.

How to manage bad reviews

Receiving positive reviews is a real boost. For someone you don't know from Adam and who may be on the other side of the world to leave you a 5-star review on Amazon really makes you feel that all your hard work was worth it.

But, luckily or unluckily, sooner or later someone is going to give you a bad review. It's life, but don't worry – **it's not always a bad thing**:

1. They show you're selling. The best way to ensure you don't receive any bad reviews is not to sell a single copy of your book. I'm sorry to tell you that, if you follow the steps in this guide, that's not going to happen. Authors who sell well or very well are going to get bad reviews, so unless you get more bad than good, BE HAPPY ABOUT THEM.

2. They give you credibility. A book with only positive reviews can sometimes seem not real. Having a negative review in there helps convince your potential readers that the other reviews are genuine.

3. They give you the chance to improve. Of course, if the review doesn't say much more than "your book sucks" or "I didn't like it", it's not awfully useful — but if you come across one explaining exactly what the reader didn't like, it gives you the chance to review that part of the book and improve or even remove it if you think that you should. Pay special attention to multiple comments mentioning the same thing.

Now that you've discovered the positive side of a negative review, let's look at how to handle it when they appear:

1. Keep perspective. I know, through my own experience and that of my clients, that your first impulse when you get a bad review is to get mad if you know your book is fantastic or to get depressed if you were already questioning your own work. Neither of these two states of mind will help you tackle the situation the way you should, so it's very important to keep perspective. Firstly, remember that a bad review isn't always a negative thing – as we just looked at – and secondly, I recommend that you think of your favorite book. Find it on Amazon and scroll to its reviews. Surprised? Who could have imagined that that amazing book that changed your life could have so many negative reviews underneath it? I bet that bad review that's been keeping you up at night doesn't seem so serious now.

2. Categorize your reviews. I advise you to try to include the review in each of the following 3 categories, as we will act differently depending on each one: constructive, useless or malicious.

- **Constructive: use these to improve**. As we have seen, if the review contains useful information and explains what drove the reader to leave a negative comment, you can use it to update and improve on future editions of your book.

- **Useless: ignore these**. If they do not give us any information but simply complain without making a point, the best thing you can do is to ignore it and keep doing what you do: sell books.

- **Malicious: report these to Amazon**. If a review is offensive or you notice something suspicious in it that makes you think that it was left by your competition with the sole aim of reducing your overall rating, you can report it to Amazon and request its deletion. To do this, all you have to do is click the "report abuse" button just below it.

Once you've reached this point, you have all the tools you need to guarantee that your book becomes a true longseller that will keep on selling without you needing to lift a finger.

Does this mean that you can just lay in a hammock and wait for those thousand monthly dollars to come rolling in?

Well... there may be situations where this happens (several of my students achieved this in their first month after launch, without needing to do anything else), but I'm sorry to tell you that this is usually more down to a stroke of luck than anything else, especially outside of the US market (where it does happen often).

The truth is that for the vast majority, **earnings will consist of around $170 to $350 a month**, and this is if you do things right and according to everything I've said so far: if not, your income will likely be much closer to $0 than to $170.

HOLD UP! That's not what you promised! I hear you say.

Calm down.

Although this is all you can expect to learn from other books, in the best-case scenario, with this book... **we're just getting started**.

The DTP method: $1000 a month guaranteed

You may not know this, but this book originated in a *crowdfunding*[12] campaign on Kickstarter (if you're curious, you can take a look at it here: *soykevinalbert.com/kickstarter*).

Although it was a real success and I had no trouble reaching my funding goal, there were many people – writers included – who accused me both privately and publicly of being a liar and a scammer. This was because they believed that it wasn't possible to guarantee $1000 a month with just one book, especially in under a year.

---

[12] Crowdfunding is a collective funding model where various people from all over the world contribute small or large amounts to help make a project happen.

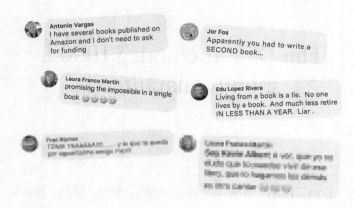

Real public comments during my crowdfunding campaign.

Among the authors who accused me of being a charlatan, there were **even some who acknowledged that they made $1000 a month** (or much more) from one of their books, but others where they barely broke $170.

This is a fact: some books will sell better than others.

To give you an example, an acquaintance of mine has several published books and, while most of them don't bring in $1000 a month, one in particular generates over $17,000 for him every month. He himself acknowledges that he doesn't know what's so special about that book, and attributes its success to luck.

Of course, this could happen to you too, and you could start earning not just 1000 but over 10,000 dollars right from the start, with barely any effort required. But just like this guy, it would be a matter of luck, and I can't help you with that. If what you're looking to do is hit the jackpot, you'd better stick to the lottery.

Where I can help you is by **guaranteeing $1000 a month**.

How is this possible? Didn't I just say in the previous chapter that earnings would usually hit around $170 and $350 a month? Am I running away with myself here?

Not at all – this is where MY METHOD comes into play. You can call it *The Kevin Method for Writers and Non-Writers of Non-Fiction Who Want to Live Off Their Books and Tell Their Bosses to Go to Hell...* or you could call it the DTP Method: Divide, Translate, Promote.

With this method, you'll keep leaving it up to fate whether you hit the jackpot and earn $10,000 or more from just one book without having to do anything, but you'll guarantee that $1000 a month by applying these three simple strategies.

Strategy nº 1: **divide.**

As I just explained, some of the authors who wrote to me during my crowdfunding campaign admitted that, although they made good money from some of their books, others didn't break $170. Through my own experience and that of my colleagues and clients, I can say it's rare for a book to give you less than that if you've done your job properly (the steps I've explained to you so far). However, we are going to be pessimistic just for a moment: let's imagine that, once you launch your book, you only make $100 a month.

I think that even those who wrote to me to call me a scammer and a liar would agree that **you can guarantee $100 a month**.

If you sell your book at $19.99, your royalties per book will come in at around $10[13]. This means that if you sell ten books, a month, you're

---

[13] This will depend according to number of pages: the more pages, the lower the royalties (if the sale price is the same).

already at $100. And bear in mind that, for reasons of simplicity, I'm not including the royalties from your book's digital version in this, and these will often be lower than for the physical version.

Do you think you can get ten measly sales a month from a bookstore (Amazon) that has over 300 million users? Easy, right?

Let's keep going!

I'm sure that, in your first book, you tried to condense all the knowledge and experience you've accumulated over the years, and write a book to be proud of. That's commendable, and the sensation of self-realization is incomparable, but that doesn't mean that a fat tome with a gazillion chapters will sell more than a slim little book that focuses on just one of those chapters.

Did you know that books of between 5000 and 15,000 words are trending on Amazon, and that they are selling very, very well?

Readers – particularly of non-fiction – are searching more and more for books that get straight to the point, bringing solutions to their problems in a brief and concise way that can be consumed in a single sitting. So much so that Amazon has created a special category just for them: short reads.

I think you see where I'm going with this.

What if you were to divide your book into chapters – the most important ones – and publish them separately, as short reads or mini-books?

Imagine that, in addition to publishing your book, you publish another five mini-books made up of the five most important chapters from your first. The number of shorter books you can publish will depend in part on the length of the main one, of course, but I'm sure you won't find it hard to extract five good chapters that could work on their own.

With this simple strategy, you will have **multiplied the profits from your book by six,** when in reality... **they're the same book, just in instalments!**

- Main book = $100/month
- Mini-book 1 = $200 ($100/month x 2)
- Mini-book 2 = $300 ($100/month x 3)
- Mini-book 3 = $400 ($100/month x 4)
- Mini-book 4 = $500 ($100/month x 5)
- Mini-book 5 = $600 ($100/month x 6)

You may be wondering: can a mini-book be sold at the same price as the main one? Well, it can, but it's not the norm, nor do I recommend it. But can it sell as many copies as the main one? Of course – and with a reduced price, among other things, I promise you'll sell a lot more of them.

Even with a lower price, the important thing is that your profits are ultimately the same from the shorter books as from the long one.

Example:

Main book .... 10 sales x $10 = $100
Mini-books .... 20 sales x $5 = $100

Can you think of a faster way to multiply your income from your book?

Think about it: even in the best-case scenario in which you apply my *Writer in 30 Days* method[14], writing a good book will involve several weeks of work. But **dividing it up will only take a few hours**.

Not convinced by the idea of chopping up your book? I understand – at first, I couldn't see it, either. I thought that it meant selling incomplete

---

[14] Explained in the *first part of Successful Self-Publishing*: soykevinalbert.com/ssp1

books, when it was really about selling **super-specific or specialized books,** and they were very well received by readers.

Once you change your perspective, a new world of possibilities will open up before your eyes.

7 hidden benefits of dividing up your book

1. It increases your authority.

If you think publishing a bestseller in your chosen field gives you authority, imagine what several under your personal brand can do for you. People will perceive you as more of an expert if you have ten published books than if you just have one, even though it's really the same thing!

2. Better reach and visibility.

When you divide your book into several miniature ones, you will have the chance to use specific keywords for each of them. This, among other things, will enable you to try **as many different titles as mini-books** that you decide to publish, and as you now know, *a book's title is the n° 1 secret to getting discovered on Amazon.*

By doing this, you will be multiplying your chances of being found by your potential readers.

3. There's something for everyone.

You may think that if you write a book on a given topic, you are writing the perfect book for everyone interested in that subject. However, some people prefer to read a more specific book that focuses on a single point or idea.

By dividing up your book, you will be creating the perfect book for a higher number of people, increasing your sales.

4. There's something for every budget.

Although a book is a relatively low-cost item, there are people who find it hard to stump up, say, $29 for a tome that only contains one chapter that interests them – especially by an author they don't know yet.

Mini-books enable readers to pay less because they focus on just one point or chapter from the main book.

Since the investment needed is less, more readers will decide to give you a chance – and if they like what they read, they will be much more likely to end up buying the other mini-books in the series, especially if you put in a good introduction to the next one at the end of each of them.

You are offering readers the chance to buy your book in affordable instalments.

5. More income.

Let's say you decide to sell your main book for $19.99 (a relatively high price for a book, regardless of its length) and your mini-books for $9.99 each (a pretty low price, even for a short read).

If you divided your main book into five and a reader ends up buying them all – which is highly likely – then instead of making $19.99 on your main book, you will have made $49.95! Two and a half times more!

6. More lottery tickets.

I really don't like to rely on luck, especially when it comes to my finances. That's why I created this system where I guarantee at least $1000 a month for each book. But this doesn't mean that, if the gods of fate smile on one of my books and it starts generating $10,000 a month without me knowing how or why (just like what happened to my friend), I can start jumping up and down with joy. If I get that stroke of luck, then that's great, of course.

Well, by dividing your book up into several mini-books, you're effectively buying more "lottery tickets" and increasing your chances of your number coming up.

7. Motivation.

After the fact that **dividing your book will multiply your income,** this is my second favorite benefit when you're still in the process of writing your book.

Whether you're still finishing your book or you haven't started it yet, I recommend that you do the following: instead of writing it in full and then dividing it up and publishing, **start publishing the mini-books as you go along,** and then when you finish all of them, publish the main book.

I promise that seeing your mini-books start selling and generating income will give you the motivation you need to finish your book, and you won't end up like the millions of authors who start their books but never finish them.

I hope that with all the benefits – both to you and to your readers – that I've told you about, you're motivated to try this extraordinary strategy that will make things really easy for you when it comes to reaching your $1000 goal.

All that's left is to look at...

How to divide a book.

Once you change your way of thinking and start looking at mini-books as super-specialized books that have great value for readers by providing specific solutions to specific problems, you will be able to think of dozens of ways to divide up your book. You could create series of short readers from the sections of your main book, others from its chapters, or you may even realize that certain points you make are better expressed in individual books (that aren't part of a series) with just a small mention of those points in the main book, and so on.

To help make this clearer and hopefully inspire you, I'm going to show you the (provisional) division and publication plan for my main book: *Living Off Your Book*.

This was the initial contents page I intended to include:

1. WRITE YOUR BOOK

Chap. 1 – Why write a book?

Chap. 2 – Excuses and writer's block

Chap. 3 – What to write

Chap. 4 – The title

Chap. 5 – How to write your book

    5.1. The magic of mind maps

    5.2. The power of research

    5.3. The structure of your blueprint

Chap. 6 – Challenge: Writer in 30 Days

2. PUBLISH YOUR BOOK

Chap. 7 – Self-publishing vs publishing house

Chap. 8 – Editing

Chap. 9 – Layout

Chap. 10 – Cover

Chap. 11 – Description

Chap. 12 – Keywords

Chap. 13 – Categories

Chap. 14 – Pricing

Chap. 15 – Upload your book to Amazon

3. SELL YOUR BOOK

Chap. 16 – Bestseller in 24 hours

Chap. 17 – From bestseller to longseller

Chap. 18 – Reviews

Chap. 19 – Your retirement book

    19.1. Strategy nº 1: divide

    19. 2. Strategy nº 2: translate

    19. 3. Strategy nº 3: promote

Chap. 20 – Amazon Ads

Chap. 21 – Facebook Ads

Chap. 22 – Audiobook

Chap. 23 – Crowdfunding

Chap. 24 – Preorder on Amazon

Chap. 25 – Relaunch your book

How many mini-books could you get out of all this? So far, I plan to get 12 books from my original one. And I'm sure that many new ideas for mini-books will come up along the way:

1. Mini-book: *Write Your Book* ($4.99)

2. Mini-book: *Publish Your Book* ($4.99)

3. Mini-book: *Sell Your Book*[15] ($6.99)

4. **Main book**: *Self-Publishing Secrets* ($9.99)

5. Mini-book: *Audiobook* ($4.99)

6. Mini-book 4: *Amazon Ads* ($9.99)

7. Mini-book 5: *Facebook Ads* ($9.99)

8. Mini-book: *Crowdfunding* ($4.99)

9. Mini-book: *Relaunch Your Book* ($4.99)

10. Mini-book: *Cover* ($1.99)

11. Mini-book: *Editing* ($1.99)

12. Mini-book: *Layout* ($1.99)

13. Mini-book: *Reviews* ($1.99)

I organized the list in the order in which I intend to publish the books, and indicated the price I intend to do it at (Kindle version).

Making a list like this in advance, with the possible division of your book into mini-books, can also ultimately give you a better version of the main one, since you won't feel the need to include absolutely everything in it purely to show how

---

[15] Turned into *Successful Self-Publishing 3*, the book you're reading right now.

much you know or to avoid leaving anything out. Some chapters, no matter how interesting, are better as standalone books, so that you can improve understanding of them and increase the value of your main book.

Pro tip: Once you have made your list, take a look at **which mini-books could work as a series**. For example, I decided to group together 1, 2 and 3 from my list in the series *Successful Self-Publishing* (write, publish and sell). This way, when you upload them to KDP, you will be able to indicate that they are a series, and Amazon will notify readers who buy one of them that there are others in the series, which will obviously improve your sales.

Considerations when dividing up a book

A little recommend for if you decide to utilize this strategy and divide your book:

Treat your mini-books with the same care as you did your main book.

Dividing a book into five short reads will take you less than a tenth of the time it would take you to write five new books, but that doesn't mean it doesn't require some work.

If you dedicated a week to preparing a good cover for your main book, took care over creating a title (and subtitle) that would enamor Amazon and your readers, put together a launch team to help you climb the ranks and get your first reviews... **you should do exactly the same with your mini-books!**

Pro tip: Use the endings of your mini-books to introduce at least one other mini-book, and add a **universal direct link** to it. This is particularly effective when the book is part of a series.

Why do I say universal link?

Many people don't know that Amazon is actually made up of a total of fourteen different online stores (*.com*, *.es*, *.fr*, etc.). This means that, if you share a link to your book on *Amazon.co.uk*, the user will be sent to the British version of the platform, and if they don't have an account there, they won't be able to buy directly.

Enter universal links.

Rather than ignoring your international readers or sharing fourteen separate links for each of Amazon's stores, you're going to create a magic link that will redirect users to your book's page in their country.

To do this, we are going to use the tool Booklinker. It couldn't be easier to use:

1. Go to *booklinker.com*.
2. Enter the URL of your book.
3. Click «Create Universal Link».

4. Personalize your universal link (with your book's title, for example).
5. Sign up.
6. That's it!

This is how the universal direct link to one of my books looks:

- **Before**:

  amazon.com/gp/product/B08R73RXT3/

  *Valid only for Amazon.es.
- **After**: *mybook.to/branding-secrets/*

  *Valid for all of Amazon's fourteen online stores.

Strategy nº 2: **translate**.

If you did a quick mental calculation in the previous chapter of the royalties my book would generate once divided into twelve parts, you will have realized that – without my doing anything else, and even with profits of $100 per month per book, which is a highly conservative estimate – I would reach and surpass my monthly goal of $1000.

But what happens if, despite trying your best to figure it out, you find that only four – not twelve – of your book's chapters warrant publication as individual books? We would be looking at "just" $500 a month. How do we get to the $1000 a month I promised you?

If you have already reached $500 a month by dividing up your book, and you don't want to (or can't find a way to) divide it up any further, what you need to do is as simple as **translating your**

book into another language... and DOUBLING YOUR INCOME.

It may seem silly because it sounds so obvious, but do you know how many authors are achieving good book sales and still haven't had them translated?

I understand that someone who has published a book and scarcely made peanuts from it will have no intention of translating it to another language just so the same thing can happen again. But I can only think of two reasons why those authors who *are* obtaining good royalties from their books might not have them translated: they don't know how to do it, or they think it's too expensive.

If this sounds like you, we're going to look at two ways of translating your books into any language, simply and even for free!

1. Upwork: my choice.

Of all the places you can look for a translator for your book, I personally recommend *Upwork*, a virtual marketplace that puts the best freelancers from around the world in touch with companies or individuals looking for talented professionals.

Basically, all you have to do is sign up to the platform and publish your job post (the translation of your book) by following the steps the website indicates. You will start receiving proposals from dozens of freelancers interested in translating your book. Your only task is to find the professional offering you the best quality/price ratio.

How to choose your translator

The best thing about working with a platform like Upwork is that you can check the profiles of all the freelancers volunteering to translate your book: their rates, training, portfolios... and most important of all, their customer reviews.

You can really get lost among so much information, and spend days checking profiles. But you don't need to. This is how I do it:

First, I discard any proposals from freelancers who have earned less than $10,000 on the platform and don't have at least 90% customer satisfaction. Just by doing this, you will reduce your list to just a few proposals. Among the professionals still standing, begin to go through them and see if any of them specialize in or have previously translated books on the same topic as yours, and mark these as favorites.

Now all that's left is to talk about rates.

How much it costs to translate a book with Upwork

The answer is simple: **however much you want to spend**.

For years now, I have used Upwork almost every week for something (you can't imagine the things you can commission there). The first thing I learned about working with these platforms is that, just like in the offline world, prices vary *to infinity and beyond.*

For the same book (let's say, thirty thousand words long), translated by two freelancers with the same level of education and experience, you can expect to pay anything between $170 and almost $700[16].

This **huge** difference depends on various factors: the main one is the country of origin of

---

[16] Official prices (recommended by the Editorial Freelancers Association) for translating a book are between $0.09 and $0.19 per word.

the freelancer, since the cost of living is different in Spain and the US, for example. But it can also depend on how in-demand or "famous" the freelancer is.

But don't be disheartened – this is the very magic of these marketplaces. Remember: if the professional has 90% customer satisfaction or more and has earned at least $10,000 on the platform, you can almost guarantee they'll do a good job.

As a guide, for my last few books, which had between fifteen and thirty thousand words each, I have paid an average of $115.

2. Babelcube: free.

Babelcube is a platform that puts writers in touch with translators. The former gets their book translated for free, and the latter take home a portion of the book's sales.

Once you've reached an agreement with a translator and the work is done, Babelcube will publish your translated book on over 300 sales channels: Amazon, Apple, Barnes & Noble...

The system for sharing royalties varies depending on the number of units sold. The more sales, the better the conditions for the author: from 30% at the start, up to 75% once $8000 has been reached.

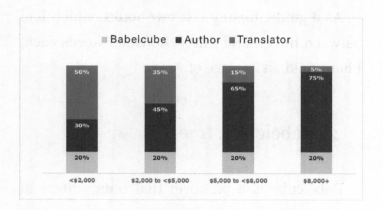

Distribution of royalties with Babelcube.

Something to bear in mind:

- Shorter books have more chance of getting a translator interested in them (since they involve less of a gamble).
- If you've had good results with your book in English, more translators will be willing to translate it.
- If no one is interested in your book when you upload it to the platform, you can contact translators directly. Babelcube offers a detailed list of its freelancers.

Advantages of Babelcube:

- Cost = $0 (you just share your earnings).
- The chance to translate your book into more than 15 languages.
- You choose your translator or team of translators.
- Sell your book on hundreds of sales channels and subscription services.
- Earn additional income in new markets.

How Babelcube works

1. Create an account. Provide as much detail as you can, as this will allow translators to get to know you. This will be your covering letter.

2. Create your book's profile. Post a profile for each book you want to have translated. Make sure you include all the information about its potential: sales history and royalties, reviews, awards and recognition (categories it has become a bestseller in) and any other information you think is relevant. It's also recommended that you include a brief extract (maximum 2000 characters) from your book, so translators can provide you with a sample translation.

3. Choose your translator. Once you have uploaded your book's profile, you will start getting offers from various translators. Often, they work in teams: one will translate, while another edits and proofreads (what a luxury).

For every proposal, they will indicate the target language and estimated timeframe. All you have to do is review the proposals, research the translators' profiles, and accept the offer from your chosen translator(s).

4. Check the translation of the first few pages. When the first ten pages have been translated, you will have an opportunity to check its quality, and if it's not good, you can cancel the job without being penalized.

Pro tip: If you don't have the necessary level of the target language to be able to check the translation (which is normal) and you don't have any friends who can give you a hand with this, you may want to create a mini-job on Upwork for around $10-15 so that another freelancer can check the sample for you.

5. Review the final translation. Once the translation is complete, you can check it and

suggest changes or modifications before approving it. If for any reason you consider that the quality is insufficient, and you can't come to an agreement with the translator, you can cancel the job but you will be charged a fee.

6. Prepare your book for distribution. Babelcube will allow you to convert your book into various formats, publish it and edit it on its different sales channels.

7. Receive your royalties. Babelcube will pay you your royalties regularly, and you can track sales and payments from your user dashboard.

Now that you know two low-cost methods for professionally translating your book, I'm sure you will have already done the math: if dividing your book into five can net you at least $500 monthly, then translating it into even just one other language will get you to the goal I set with this book: $1000 a month.

So why not translate it into more than one language?

Of course, if for any reason you have your book translated and still don't reach $500 a month (although this would be unusual), I suggest you choose another language and repeat the process. Even better, if you have reached (or thrashed) that goal, you should still **choose another language... AND DOUBLE YOUR INCOME AGAIN!**

Strategy nº 3: **promote**.

I'm sure by now you've realized that just by applying the first two strategies of the DTP method, you can pretty much keep increasing your royalties as much as you want – but before you hang that medal around your neck and consider your goal reached, let me tell you about one final strategy that can help you to increase your passive income even more. This time, it won't come from your book's profits.

As I've told you, to find a system that enabled me to guarantee my retirement fund with just one book, I invested quite a lot of money (nearly $6000) in several training courses. Among them, I bought over $1000 worth of Facebook Ads. The creator, a well-known Spanish-language guru, personally promised me that **with Facebook ads, I could earn as much as I wanted through selling my book**. I was already pretty suspicious due to other, similar courses that had caught me out before, but since the guru and I had some mutual friends – and he was offering a double refund guarantee – I eventually decided to pay for the course. As you can probably imagine, it ended up not working, and despite his double guarantee I never did get my money back.

The reason why this course was not useful for making money from a book was that, like so many other courses, it was based on what is known in marketing circles as a **value ladder**, and to make use of this strategy you need at least one *hook* (or entry-level) product and one *premium* product or service:

1. **Hook**: you offer a product at a very low price (less than $20) or even for free. Its aim is to get customers' email addresses. Usually, spending on ads to bring users to the website where they can buy or download this product will be greater than the profit made from it.

2. **Premium product**: this has a higher price ($100 and up). It is offered to users who have bought the hook product. Statistics tell us that a percentage of these customers will also buy the premium product. This is where you get your investment back on selling the entry-level product, and where profit is made.

Do you see where the problem is in this system if you're trying to make money from just one book?

- **You have to pay to sell**. Your book is considered to be the hook.
- **It assumes you have a premium product to sell**. I didn't.

That is exactly why I requested – unsuccessfully – for my money to be refunded from the Facebook Ads course: I didn't want to have to pay people to read my book, nor did I have the time or the inclination to create a premium product right then, and I'm guessing, since you're reading this book, that you're in the same boat.

But what would you say if I told you that I ended up finding a way to create a value ladder without needing to invest money in getting your book read and which you could use to sell a premium product without needing to create one?

Sounds too good to be true? Remember that in your review ;)

1. How to sell your book without investing in ads.

This part is easy – I talked about it at the beginning of this book. Given that you're going to sell your book on Amazon and not via your own website, you don't need to spend money on marketing to attract potential readers – Amazon will take care of that!

2. How to sell a premium product without needing to create one.

Now for the good part. Instead of creating a premium product, **you're going to sell someone else's** :)

This way, it won't be necessary for you to design an extraordinary product that people are prepared to dig deep for. All you have to do is find that extraordinary product and promote it... in your book itself.

You might be wondering how the hell you're supposed to make money by promoting someone else's product. Let me give you a brief introduction to **affiliate marketing**.

Affiliate marketing is a system whereby an affiliate (you) promotes the product of a person or company (the producer) in exchange for commission on every sale.

It's a fantastic commercial system where everyone's a winner:

- **The affiliate**: they can monetize their website, social media, **book**... by selling third party products without doing the work involved in creating a premium product.

- **The producer**: they get new sales without having to invest in ads.

- **The customer**: they get more channels for finding information on products, and can make better purchasing decisions. The recommendation usually comes from someone they trust (you).

What product should you promote?

Before explaining the process of becoming an affiliate, first things first: what kind of product should you promote, and where can you find it?

Although on your value ladder, the premium product wasn't created by you, you need to apply the same logic we would use if you had done. The product you promote **should be an added or complementary step to your book**. It would also be good to use a product with similar content but in another format (a video course, for example).

Taking my own book for example, I can think of a lot of products that might be of interest to people who read it: *How to Sell Your Services Using Your Book, Create a Course From Your Book, Facebook Ads For Authors, Amazon Ads For Authors, Crowdfunding For Authors, Write Your Book in 30 Days, Boost Your Personal Brand Through Your Book,...* Okay, so the titles need some work, but you get the idea, right?

I recommend that you make a list of possible courses or products that could align with your book before you begin your research.

Now that you have a few ideas for interesting products that might complement your book, it's time to find out if anyone else has already had those ideas and created courses out of them.

If you know enough about a topic to have written a book on it, I'm sure you already know the leading experts in your field and the best infoproducts on the market.

If, for some reason, you don't, you have two options:

- **Google it**. All you have to do is type in the names of the products on your list and the word "course". When you find what you're looking for, you need to find out if you can sell that product as an affiliate. I recommend that you email the course creator and ask them directly. The affiliate option is not always publicly advertised.

- **Search on Hotmart**[17]. This platform enables you to easily search through its thousands of products and filter them according to various criteria (sales commission, price, etc.). The good thing about searching on Hotmart is that, if you find a product that fits, it almost definitely has an affiliate option.

IMPORTANT: before you recommend one of these courses, you need to be sure of its quality and that it is worth what it costs. The best thing to do is recommend one you have tried yourself and liked. If you haven't done this, you have several options: buy it and do it, ask the expert to give you access to it for a few days to check it in depth, and/or research what other customers thought. Remember you're staking your reputation and credibility on this.

---

[17] Hotmart is a platform specializing in the commercialization and distribution of digital products: *hotmart.com*

If you've written a book to be proud of, don't throw your work down the drain by recommending a bad or mediocre course just to earn a few extra bucks. Even though the course isn't yours, if you're the one who recommends it in your book, your readers will end up associating it with you and what they think of the course will affect what they think of your book.

It needs to be a product that you would recommend even if you weren't earning commission on doing so: when you do this, you need to be adding value. For example, it would have cost me nothing to include an affiliate link to the Facebook Ads course I mentioned and earn around $600 for every reader who ended up buying it, but that would be unethical on my part, given that I wasn't satisfied with it myself.

How to become an affiliate

Being an affiliate of a course or product is as easy as having a personalized affiliate URL. Example:

- Normal URL: *supercurso.com*
- Affiliate URL: *supercurso.com/kevinalbert*

Both URLs lead to the same website – the user will see exactly the same thing. The only difference is that if a user ends up buying something on the website having followed the affiliate link, the affiliate will receive commission on that sale.

To get your affiliate link, all you have to do is sign up on the platform linked to the course you have decided to promote. Once you've signed up, you will be assigned an affiliate link and gain access to a control panel where you can track your sales.

Now that you have your affiliate URL, all you have to do is share it as is, or turn it into a QR code, like we looked at in the previous chapter.

Earning some extra money has never been easier.

Where should you put your affiliate link?

Given that the product you're going to promote should be a step on from your book, it makes sense for your recommendation and affiliate link to go at the end of the book. It's not just about logic – by putting it in the last few pages, you will also have more time to generate the trust you need from your reader so that your recommendation has more of an effect and a greater chance of conversion.

Be careful you don't go overboard with your final recommendation and end up making your book sound like a sales letter for the product you're promoting. Some people write books purely as tools for selling their course or someone else's. When this happens, it's obvious. Readers aren't stupid, and their dissatisfaction will be reflected in their reviews.

Your job is to recommend a product that complements your book or goes one step further. The onus of convincing a customer to buy the premium product lies with the product's creator.

Rather than using your book itself to talk about how amazing the course you're promoting is, what you can do is find a product that has a good sales page – or, even better, get an affiliate link that redirects to a webinar subscription. The conversion percentages for webinars are much higher:

- Affiliate URL> Sales page > Purchasing decision > **1-2% conversion**.

- Affiliate URL> Webinar subscription > Webinar > Sales page > Purchasing decision > **5-10% conversion**.

How much can you earn?

Now that you've chosen the perfect premium product that you want to promote, and you've included the affiliate link in your book, let's look at the numbers.

In order to get a rough estimate of the monthly commission you can earn as an affiliate, you need to know 4 things:

- **Product price**. Let's imagine the premium product you've decided to promote with your book costs $1000 (you can easily find infoproducts costing up to five times this much).

- **Commission per sale**. Out of this $1000, you take 50% - that is, $500 (50-50 is pretty normal for digital products, since they have no manufacturing costs and are pure profit).

- **Conversion percentage**. A good sales letter (your book) in the hands of a potential customer (your reader) will normally have around 2-4% conversion. This means that for every 100 books you sell, you should get around 2-4 sales[18].

- **Monthly sales of your book**. If we continue with the same numbers as above and say that, in addition to your main book (five sales per month) you have also published five mini-books on top of that (ten sales a month

---

[18] If the product is cheaper, you'll be more likely to get a sale (and vice versa).

each), you will have a total of 55 sales a month. With these numbers, you would sell between 1 and 2 premium products every month, **adding $500-1000 in affiliate commissions to the monthly royalties you get from your book.**

So, what if you have your book translated into other languages, too?

Well, then you'd be able to **multiply those affiliate commissions by the number of languages your book comes in.** That said, you would need to do some careful research into a good premium product for each of these languages.

Tip: you can create a job post on Upwork for around $10-20 to help you find a good premium product in the language you need.

CONCLUSIONS

I hope that having read through the three strategies that make up the DTP method, those $1000 that you found dubious at the start of this book now seem easily achievable (easy peasy, even).

You see now that simply by dividing your book into four more mini-books, and translating them into other languages, you can reach your goal. You can also add your affiliate link to a premium product, create even more divisions, translate them into even more languages. If you do the math, you'll see that reaching $3-5000 a month from just one book is not at all unrealistic. So...

Why did I limit myself to guaranteeing $1000 a month?

Firstly, because that was the initial goal that drove me to write this book: to equal, in just a year, the retirement pension that it took my father more than fifty years to reach.

And secondly, because I have realized that when someone discovers the true potential of a book, the DTP method takes a back burner. Why carry on dividing, translating and promoting if you've already hugely surpassed your initial goal?

Can I tell you a secret?

None of my students has managed to divide their book into more than three parts or translate it into more than one other language, and yet they have ALL reached and surpassed their goal in under a year – some even during their first month.

How is this possible?

I like to explain it with what I call *the law of the corridor*:

Imagine you're standing at the start of a long corridor, with a big door at the other end. That door would be the goal you have set yourself (let's say, $1000 monthly from your book). Given that you can see your objective – the door at the end of the corridor – you start walking toward it. But along the way, you realize that there are other doors to the side that you would never have seen if you hadn't started walking toward the door at the end. Now for the good part: since you're curious, you decide to open some of these doors (the ones that most catch your eye) and behind them you discover new or better ways to reach your goal, or ways to surpass your original objective, showing you new goals that you would never have thought of but that make you completely forget about your initial goal once you know about them.

This law, applied to the objective of this book, could translate into your book and mini-books not giving you 50 but rather 500 each, your main book reaching those $1000 monthly out of nowhere, a publishing house contacting you and offering to pay you much more than you had planned for, getting your dream job thanks to your book, Amazon offering to turn your book into an audiobook and pay you handsomely for it, deciding to create your own premium product, and so on[19]...

If, as I say, this is always (or nearly always) going to happen, why did I tell you about the DTP method?

Well, because this method is going to be responsible for you beginning to walk toward that door at the end of the corridor. Most people aren't capable of taking even that first step if they can't see the way ahead clearly and know (or think) that there is no chance they'll fail. It's human nature. With my method, I've given you the confidence that no matter what happens, even if you don't find any more doors as you walk

---

[19] All of these are real examples from clients or colleagues of mine.

down the corridor, or even if you don't like what's behind them, your main objective is guaranteed.

So, what's next?

First of all...

CONGRATULATIONS!

Only 1% of people who say they're going to write a book actually do it. But what's truly admirable is that small group of heroes (to which you belong) who, not content with having written a book, decide to take matters into their own hands and ensure that their work reaches their readers.

To recap, in this book you learned:

- How your book can help you escape the rat race.
- Why a book is the perfect business.

- How to turn your book into a bestseller in less than 24 hours.
- Why being a bestseller is worthless.
- How to turn your bestseller into a longseller that keeps on getting sales past its launch.
- Why reviews are key to a book's success or failure.
- How to get Amazon reviews continuously and legally.
- How to guarantee an income of $1000 a month from just one book.
- How to get your book translated for free.
- How to sell a premium product without having to create it.
- And more...

So, now what?

Once you've reached at least $1000 a month with your book, the possibilities are endless:

- You can turn it into an audiobook and publish it on Audible.

- You can learn Amazon marketing and boost your sales and income.
- You can hire a ghostwriter to help you write your next books... or, even better, to write them for you.
- You can train up in Facebook Ads and create a sales funnel from your own website
- You can create your own premium product and promote it in your books.
- ...

If you want to learn how to use these and many other strategies, plus all the new discoveries from my experiments and research so you can **keep increasing profits from your book,** drop me an email at _books@soykevinalbert.com_ with the subject line "Tell me more", and I'll keep you updated.

If course, if you have any doubts or want to make any comments to me personally, you can write to me at the same email address. I would love to hear from you and learn about your book.

My father (the reason this book exists) and me.

Hugs to you, fellow author!

Kevin Albert

Important

Like all my books, this is a beta version, meaning that just like me (that's right, I'm a beta male), it will keep improving with time and experience. To make this happen, **your opinion is essential**.

Please, leave me an Amazon review and let me know what you thought. What did you like best? Was there anything missing? Would you add anything, or take anything away?

Scan and leave a review